EASY PIANO

RAGTIME PIANO

SIMPLY AUTHENTIC

ARRANGED BY BILL IRWIN

ISBN 978-1-4584-1698-8

In Australia Contact:
Hal Leonard Australia Pty. Ltd.
4 Lentara Court
Cheltenham, Victoria, 3192 Australia
Email: ausadmin@halleonard.com.au

HAL•LEONARD®
CORPORATION
7777 W. BLUEMOUND RD. P.O. BOX 13819 MILWAUKEE, WI 53213

Visit Hal Leonard Online at
www.halleonard.com

CONTENTS

BEES-WAX RAG

By HARRY J. LINCOLN
Arranged by Bill Irwin

Moderately

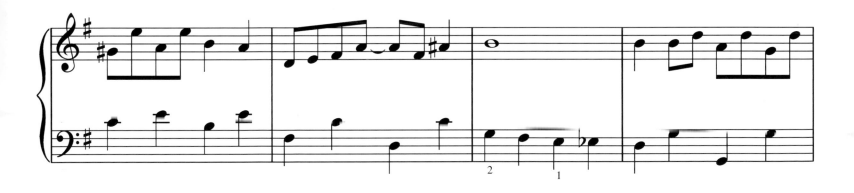

D.S. al Fine
(with repeat)

BILLIKIN RAG

By E.J. STARK
Arranged by Bill Irwin

Moderately

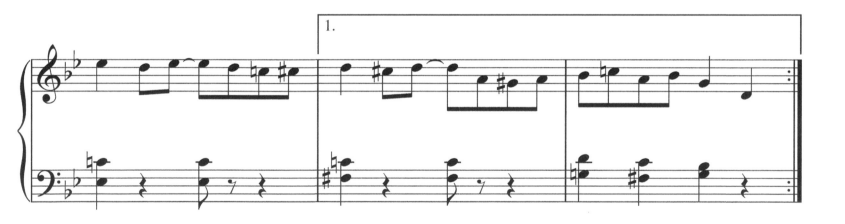

D.S. al Coda
(with repeat)

CODA

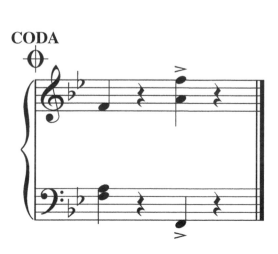

THE "BOLO" RAG

By ALBERT GUMBLE
Arranged by Bill Irwin

Moderately

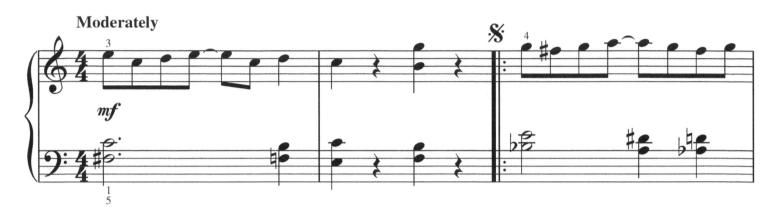

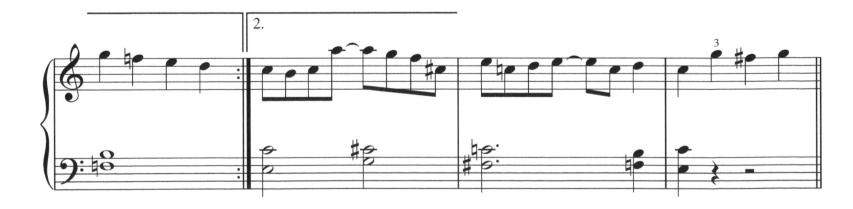

CHILI-SAUCE

By H.A. FISCHLER
Arranged by Bill Irwin

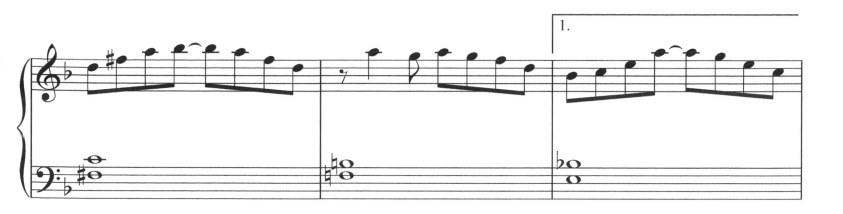

THE CHRYSANTHEMUM

By SCOTT JOPLIN
Arranged by Bill Irwin

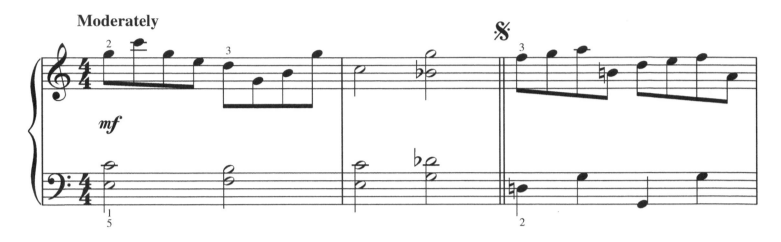

Fine

D.S. al Fine

CRIMSON RAMBLER RAG

By HARRY AUSTIN TIERNEY
Arranged by Bill Irwin

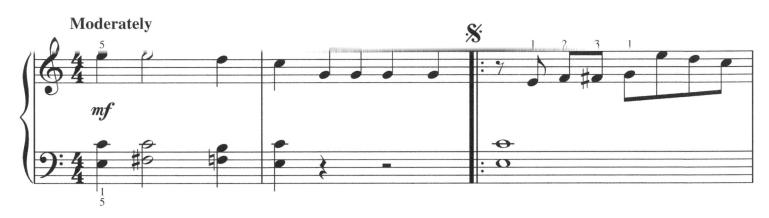

To Coda ⊕

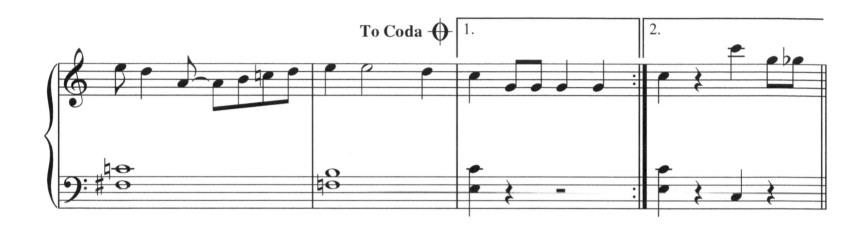

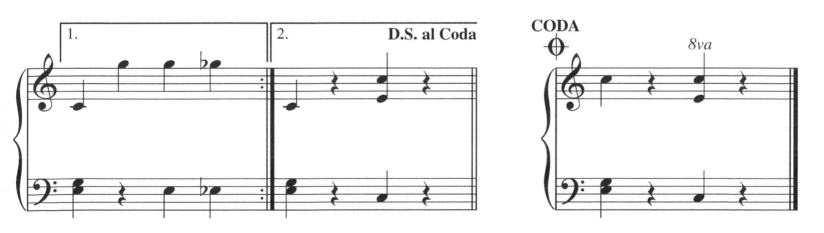

COTTON TIME

By CHAS. N. DANIELS
Arranged by Bill Irwin

Moderately

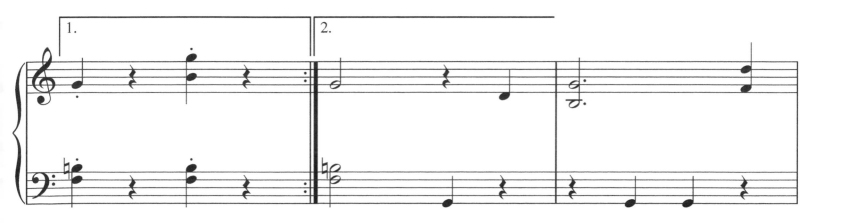

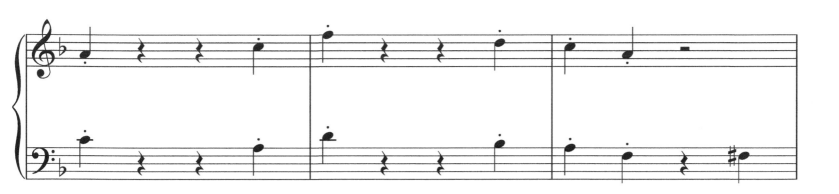

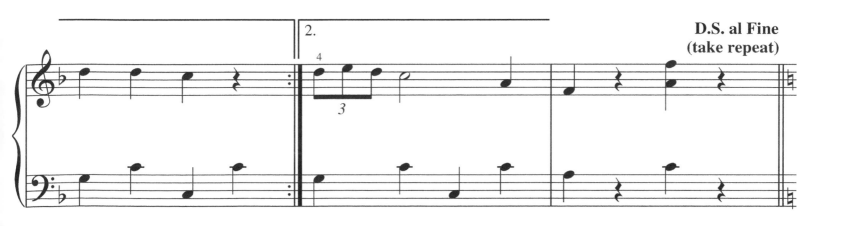

CRAB APPLES

By PERCY WENRICH
Arranged by Bill Irwin

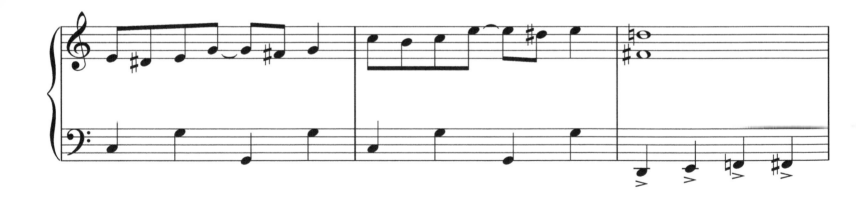

DILL PICKLES

By CHARLES JOHNSON
Arranged by Bill Irwin

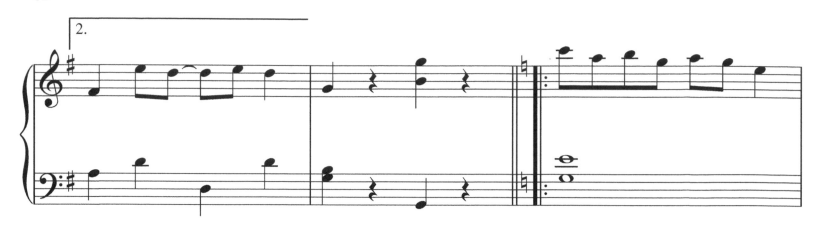

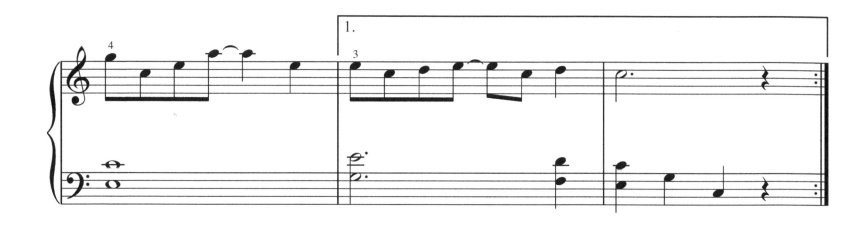

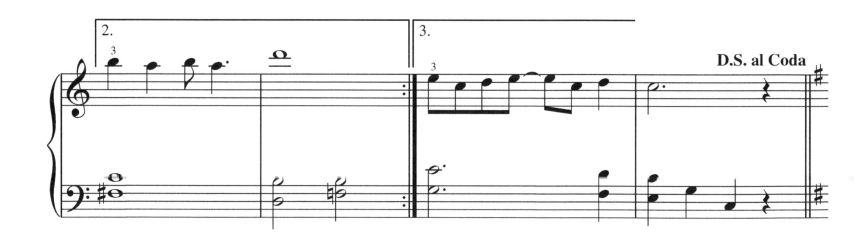

DIXIE QUEEN

By BOB HOFFMAN
Arranged by Bill Irwin

36

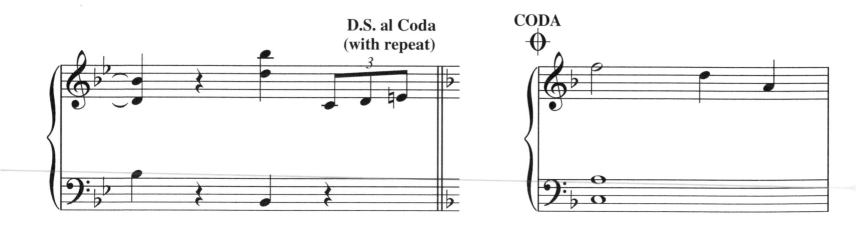

D.S. al Coda
(with repeat)

CODA

ELITE SYNCOPATIONS

By SCOTT JOPLIN
Arranged by Bill Irwin

To Coda ⊕

D.S. al Coda

CODA

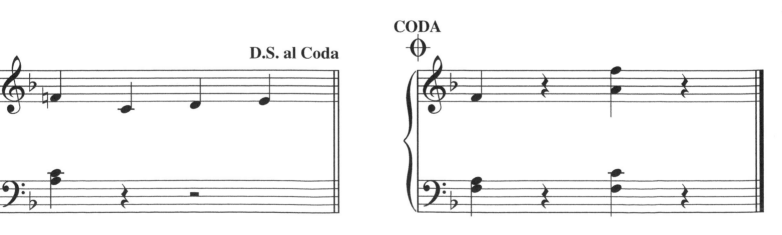

THE ENTERTAINER

By SCOTT JOPLIN
Arranged by Bill Irwin

To Coda

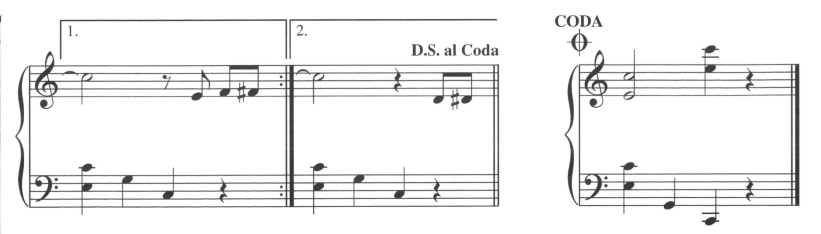

1.

2.

D.S. al Coda

CODA

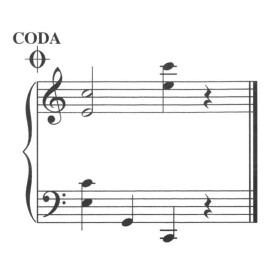

HAUNTING RAG

By JULIUS LENZBERG
Arranged by Bill Irwin

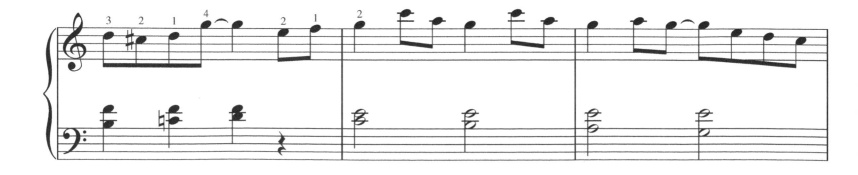

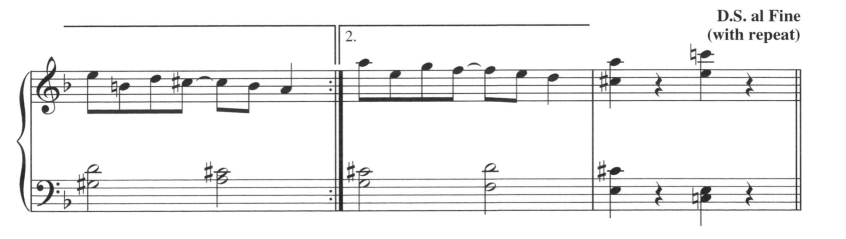

JOHNSON RAG

Words by JACK LAWRENCE
Music by GUY HALL and HENRY KLEINKAUF
Arranged by Bill Irwin

To Coda $\oplus$

D.S. al Coda
(with repeat)

CODA
$\oplus$

PEACHERINE RAG

By SCOTT JOPLIN
Arranged by Bill Irwin

THE TEMPTATION RAG

By HENRY LODGE
Arranged by Bill Irwin

POWDER RAG

By RAYMOND BIRCH
Arranged by Bill Irwin

D.S. al Coda
(take repeat)

CODA

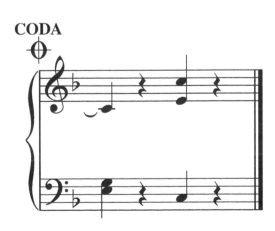

SLEEPY SIDNEY

By ARCHIE W. SCHEU
Arranged by Bill Irwin

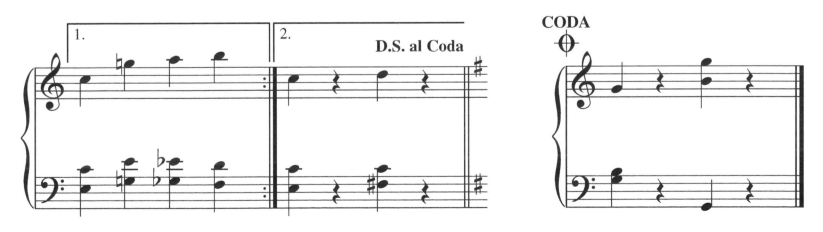

THE SMILER RAG

By PERCY WENRICH
Arranged by Bill Irwin

D.S. al Fine
(with repeat)

TIGER RAG

Attributed to D.J. LaROCCA
Arranged by Bill Irwin

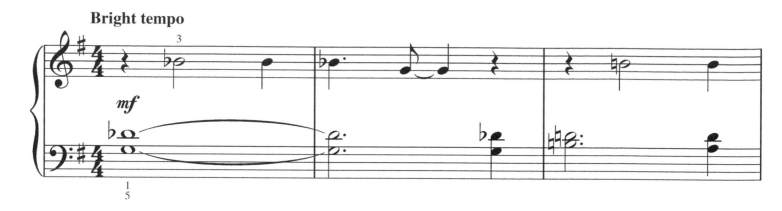

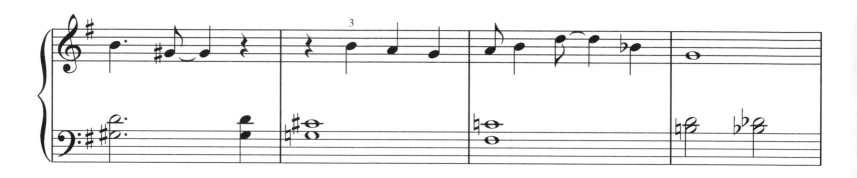

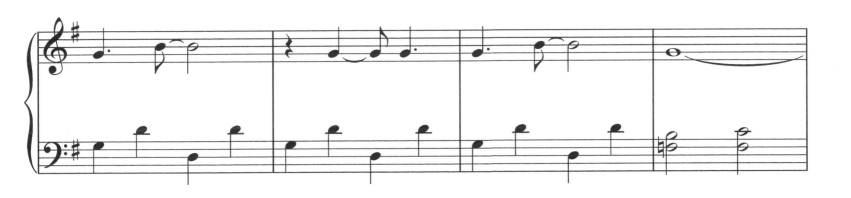

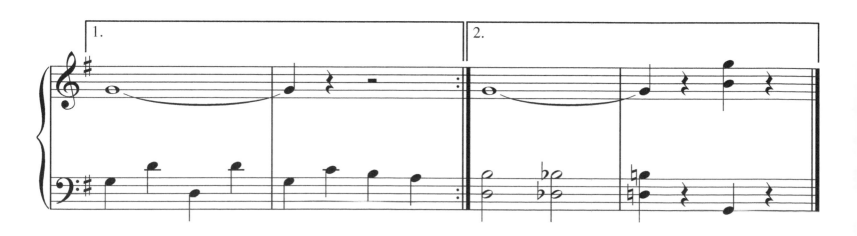

TOO MUCH MUSTARD

By CECIL MACKLIN
Arranged by Bill Irwin

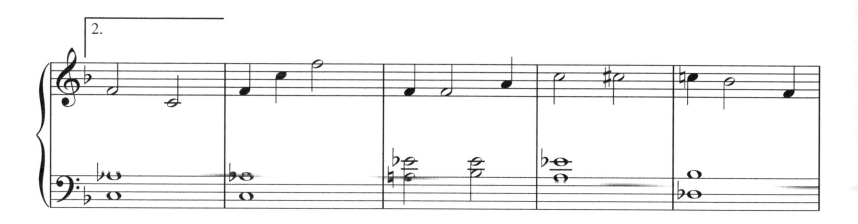

D.S. al Fine
(with repeats)

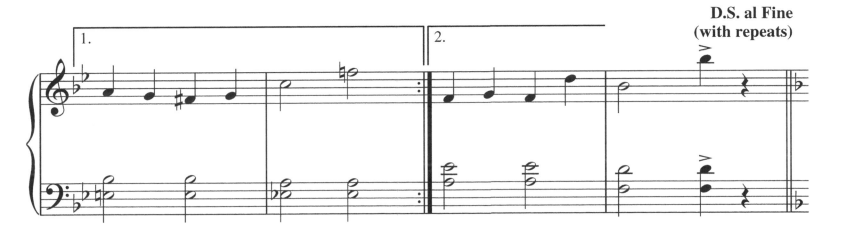

TWELFTH STREET RAG

By EUDAY L. BOWMAN
Arranged by Bill Irwin

Moderately bright

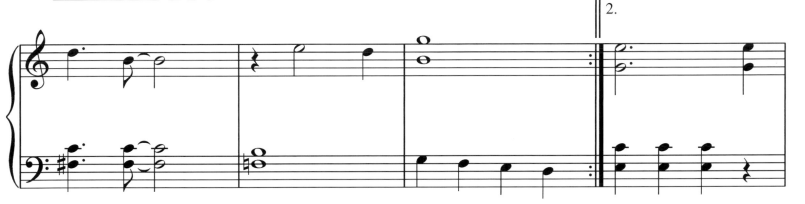

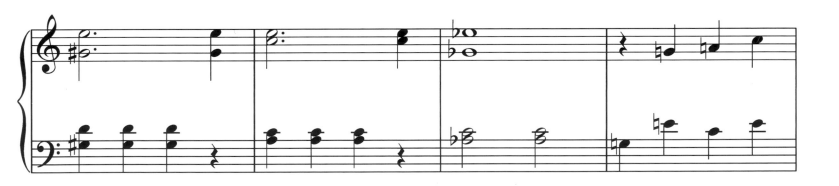

WILD CHERRIES RAG

By TED SNYDER
Arranged by Bill Irwin